New &
Improved!

New & Improved!

25 Ways to Be

More Creative and

More Effective

Pam Grout

SkillPath Publications
Mission, Kansas

Editor: Kelly Scanlon
Cover and Book Design: Rod Hankins
Cover Illustration: Steve Shamburger

Library of Congress Catalog Card Number: 95-68999
ISBN: 1-878542-78-8

10 9   8   7   6   5   4   3   97   98   99

Printed in the United States of America

Contents

1

Introduction: What's All the Fuss About Creativity?

"Why should we all use our creative power ... Because there is nothing that makes people so generous, joyful, lively, bold and compassionate, so indifferent to fighting and the accumulation of objects and money."

—*Brenda Ueland*

1

*M*ost of us assume creativity means taking up the pen or paintbrush. We think it's a quality that only sculptors, novelists, or people who wear berets possess. In truth, creativity can mean anything from making a paycheck last the required two weeks when your mortgage and your car insurance are due to a new innovation on a sales call. If you've ever looked at some of the under-bridge shanties rigged up by homeless people, you know that creativity isn't reserved for architects or the rich and famous.

But is it practical in business?

Creativity is a quality businesses are finally starting to value. In the old school of management, there was a clear delineation between managers, who "made the rules," and everyone else, who "followed them." Many managers shared Archie Bunker's style. One of his classic lines was: "When I want your opinion, Edith, I'll give it to you."

There wasn't much room for something as dangerous as creativity. Managers were bogged down in the tyranny of reason.

Give me logic, they said.

Sure, logic always leads to a solution, but is it the best solution or the most inspired? According to creativity experts, there are hundreds of solutions to most problems. And businesses that stop at the first solution are headed for trouble.

Today, most forward-thinking companies value creativity. Take Bill Arnold, chief executive at an 814-bed hospital in Nashville, Tennessee, for example. When he first took the job, he made a point of his open-door policy by hanging the actual door to his office in the lobby. He not only uses creativity in his own affairs, he also rewards his employees for being creative. He encourages them to come up with new and different ways to do things. And for those who still argue that creativity has no place in the office, hear this. In the first year of the new creativity policy, Arnold's staff decreased collections from an average 90 days past due to a respectable 48.

3M, a company that has long been recognized for its innovative products, has always extolled creativity. Upper management appreciates the fact that creativity takes time. In fact, employees are encouraged to use company time to create. As much as 15 percent of clocked-in time can be used for non-job-related work. Some of the products that have come out of this rather unique policy are Post-It notes and 3-D magnetic recording tape.

Today many companies spend millions to bring in creativity experts.

Gillette, for example, brought in one such expert to help launch a new shampoo. Executives, willing to step out of the old logic model, played games, acted wacky, toned up their creativity. In one game, each of the key managers pretended to be a strand of hair. Some "hairs" wanted more body. Others didn't want to mess around with conditioner. The result of this rather offbeat experiment was Silkience, one of the ten top-selling shampoos of 1980.

People at the top are finally starting to acknowledge that people at the "bottom" can be creative. Corning, for example, invited workers to design their new workspace when the company moved into a new plant in Erwin, New York. The workers opted for large open spaces, a high sound-dampening ceiling, and lots of windows. They designed the production line so that all the work teams were within earshot of one another. And they set up a system that allowed employees to rotate through jobs each week and earn higher pay for each new skill they learned.

What happened? Defects dropped from 10,000 parts

per million to 3 parts per million. At last report, no customer had returned any product since July 1990.

But even if your company still considers creativity a threat, this book will show you plenty of ways to be creative in your own life. All you have to do is honor the part of you that's creative and give it a little airtime.

2

Creativity— You've Got It, But Where Is It Hiding?

"The thing is to become a master and in your old age to acquire the courage to do what children did when they knew nothing."

—*Henry Miller*

7

*M*ost of us think creativity is finite, reserved for a talented few. We believe it's doled out at birth to the Picassos, the Mozarts, the Frank Lloyd Wrights of the world. The rest of us (sigh!) are fated to be *consumers* of creativity—decorating our foyers with other people's sculptures, watching other people's visions on a giant screen, and reading other people's ideas on how to sell products, to be better managers.

But the truth is, we are all creative. We all have the ability to create new ideas, solve baffling problems, even produce art. It's just that most of us have allowed our natural creativity to be smothered by a long list of self-negating assumptions:

> "I'm not good enough."
>
> "People would think I'm stupid."
>
> "I'll look like a fool."
>
> "I could never do that."

After so many years of constant smothering, we've forced our brains to shut down the part that comes up with original ideas. We've put a muzzle on that "naughty kid" who wants to color memos green or perform daring wheelies in the new rolling desk chair. After all, why bother if we're only going to be chastised and put down? Unfortunately, it's that "naughty little kid" who also produces great works of art, new ideas for selling products, and revolutionary plans for streamlining the office.

Think back to when you were a kid. The whole world was your palette. With one flip of the imagination button, Popsicle sticks turned into magical airplanes that did flips and flew upside down. A bar of soap was the Little Engine That Could ("I think I can! I think I can!") or a limousine for an infamous FBI spy. And the beach—oh, the beach—offered infinite building material. Remember the sand castle you built with moats, kings, ladies-in-waiting, and even a wizard? Back then, your imagination had no limits.

But then parents piped in:

> "Act your age."

> "Quit acting silly."

> "Do something sensible."

And then teachers had to throw in their two cents:

> "Paint between the lines."

> "Everybody knows trees are green—not purple."

> "Make an ashtray like everybody else."

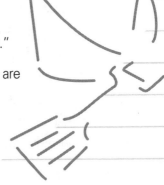

10

And then, just before you could do something really dangerous, your professors taught you about "real" art and literature, about metaphors and style. You finally realized how trivial your creative efforts were—after all, you may have thought, "Who am I, compared to the great masters?"

At work, it got worse. Unless you were the boss—the big, big cheese—your main job was to follow the rules. Hold the imagination. Besides, with overtime hours, kids to feed, and a mortgage, you probably didn't have time to play with bars of soap and sand castles anyway.

Before long, you realized you didn't even know how anymore. Alas, life's colors dimmed, its mysteries ran dry. Your capacity to wonder, to be surprised, to be puzzled was long gone, buried in a box with your childhood Tinkertoys. Some like to call this adulthood. Being responsible.

It's actually more like a lobotomy—self-imposed surgery on most of what's naturally fun. All that remains in some of our adult brains is what scientists call the left side. This is the censor, the editor, the parent who shuts down the

New and Improved!

child in us before we can really get carried away. Creativity, adulthood leads us to believe, is a useless pursuit, a childish whim, a waste of time.

To the left brain, anything unknown is perceived as wrong and possibly dangerous. It much prefers chairs arranged neatly in rows, cooperative ants marching a straight line. This is what being an adult is about. Isn't it?

If this sounds like somebody you know—maybe you?—take heart. This self-imposed lobotomy can be reversed. Our creativity, fortunately, is never lost completely. It might be submerged. It might be hiding in the basement. You might not have used it since you wrote an Easter poem for your Aunt Lana back in second grade. But it's there. Desperate for some attention. Eager to be dusted off and put back into commission.

The good news is that it's impossible to alienate your muse forever.

No matter how deeply your creativity is buried, this book will show you how to zero in and find it again. Just know that if you're still breathing, it's not too late.

3

Unleashing Your Creativity

"Trying to pin down creativity is like trying to nail Jell-O to the wall."

—Hallmark executive

13

*C*reativity—sometimes called the right brain—is our inventor, our child, our very own personal absent-minded professor. It's the part of each of us that says, "Hey! That's really cool." It puts odd things together. It's associative and freewheeling. It makes connections out of things that have never been made before. Like carriages and motors, which as Henry Ford can tell you, become cars.

Many believe that being creative is our true nature and that any blocks to our creativity are simply an unnatural thwarting of a process that's at once as normal and as miraculous as the unfolding of a green leaf in springtime.

Those who aren't blocked—those "geniuses" who use creativity—are the first to tell you that creativity is an ongoing flow that is always available, always ready. It's nothing you invent. It's more like dipping into a river.

The secret is using it on a regular basis, letting the flow come naturally.

New and Improved!

In the past, you may have relied on a hit-and-run approach to creativity. With discipline, creative flow becomes more like eavesdropping and less like freeing a Tasmanian devil. But it takes time—and it takes commitment.

Don't Have to Be Michaelangelo

Part of the problem is that creativity, like everything else, has become compartmentalized. It's something assigned to specialists. Why make up a song when you can flick on a radio and listen to somebody who *knows* how to sing? Why paint a picture when you can go to the museum and observe *real* painters? For that matter, why try to do anything at all when you can just as easily hit a button on a remote control and watch other people's scripts played out on television.

How many times have you heard—or maybe even said:

"I'm just not creative."

"Sister Mary Margaret told me I should stick with math."

"The tests proved it. I flunked grade school art."

Discard all of it. Research has proven conclusively that 99.9 percent of us were born with rich and vigorous imaginations and that creativity is universally distributed. In fact, we all create all the time. It's just that some of us are creating things that really don't serve us. Things like apathy, boredom, lethargy.

All of us have creativity bottled up inside, waiting to get out. Creativity can be learned, strengthened, enhanced, and effectively applied in everyday living.

But it's not always easy making contact with your muse. Everyday concerns often interfere. Old parental tapes drown it out. Lack of exercise has made it flabby.

So how do you make up to your muse?

It's really simple. Give it a voice. Let it out.

Yes, the secret is practice.

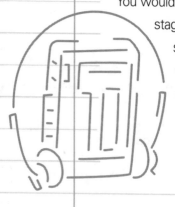

You wouldn't expect a concert pianist to walk on stage without rehearsing. Beethoven's symphonies may sound like a piece of cake for Toscanini, but don't be fooled. He spent hours upon hours in practice—first honing the skills of piano playing in general and then working on specific pieces.

Your brain needs to be pumped up. It's just sitting there, waiting for a jumpstart.

In the past, it may not have occurred to you to work on your mind—on your creative problem-solving skills or your artistic abilities. Maybe, like many other people, you figured you either had them or you didn't.

But just like any skill—from blacksmithing to paragliding—creative thinking can be mastered with even a tiny bit of concentrated effort.

Practice cracks the code. Read it again: practice. Simple practice. Simple dedication to devoting at least part of your day to your mind. Make it a priority. You don't have to allot hours. In fact, your mind is so eager to perform its inherent function that it will shape up a lot faster than a tennis swing or a volleyball serve, which, by the way, are not inherent human traits.

Consider this. We schedule time to exercise our bodies. We invest thousands of dollars on the outside of our heads (hairstyling, makeup, etc.), but it usually doesn't occur to us to exercise what's inside our heads.

Just like the bicep that gets bigger with every pump of the iron, your brain works better, functions more smoothly, if it is exercised. Scientists have proven that brain patterns are physiologically changed when worked out. Practice and discipline are the keys.

Why Develop Creativity?

When given the chance, creativity provides a thrilling sense of aliveness and connection that enriches you and everyone around you. Consider these benefits of tuning in to your creative nature:

- Besides the fact that you'll be happier, more joyful, more playful, you'll be better able to adapt to change. In this day and age, with change occurring in nanoseconds, being able to adjust is a valuable asset. Change and creativity are practically synonymous.

- Creativity will also help you discard old programs, attitudes, and habitual ways of doing things that are no longer appropriate.

All of us get stuck in old patterns. We eat the same things for breakfast. We follow the same routes to work. We react the same way when our boss calls us into the office, or when our spouse wants to talk.

When you operate from a creative mind-set, you soon realize that old habits are simply ruts that haven't received a dose of creative input yet. If you don't believe you have lots of habits, try this exercise. Just fold your arms. Now look at which arm is on top. Okay, now try to fold it the other way.

Enough said.

• Creativity reawakens your sense of experimentation and play. A task that used to be humdrum suddenly becomes fun and exciting. By applying creative principles to even mundane things like washing the car, all of life can become exciting and meaningful.

- Creativity gives you a sense of accomplishment, well-being, and purpose. Once your mind is active and alive, you'll enjoy using your creative muscle as much as you enjoy skiing or playing golf.

- Creativity makes work easier, more interesting, and more successful.

4

Getting Out of Your Own Way: Overcoming the Six Major Blocks to Creativity

"I never take counsel of my fears."

—*General George Patton*

21

22

*I*n this chapter, you're going to try to uncover the six major fears that block your creativity. You're going to get in touch with why you've shut down that natural, spontaneous urge to express yourself. Each day, you'll be asked to do something a little out of the ordinary. Do as many of the exercises as necessary to move past each block and beyond your current comfort zone. If you feel you can't do what's suggested, ask yourself why, realizing that your resistance is a block that's in the way of complete creative flow.

Don't beat yourself up over feeling some resistance. In fact, throw a party to honor yourself for finally getting in touch with the part of you that's been holding you back. Or go shopping, or treat yourself to dinner at your favorite restaurant. After all, how can you change something until you realize it needs to be changed? Like an

Indian yogi once said, How can you ask for directions unless you know where you are? It's no blot on your personality, no red letter on your soul. It's merely something to recognize. Once you do, ask yourself, "Do I want to stay that way?"

After you've performed your task, look at the block that you've leaped, and if it was easy, go on to the next exercise. If you simply couldn't go through with it, try some of the easier exercises to help you strengthen your creative muscle. Go back later and try the exercises that were at first too big a leap for you.

Block #1:

The "What Will the Neighbors Think?" Syndrome
A.K.A. The fear of appearing ridiculous

> **"What doesn't kill me makes me stronger."**
>
> —*Albert Camus*

How many times have you had a good idea, only to keep it to yourself out of fear that you'd look like a crackpot? And then, hours, days, months later, somebody else came up with the very same idea and was proclaimed a genius.

C.W. Metcalf, a humor consultant to many Fortune 500 companies, says that this fear of appearing foolish is crippling. It literally squelches joy, humor, and all creativity.

His prescription for overcoming what he calls a "debilitating disease" was to force himself to do absurd things like walking through airports minus a sock and shoe. Or to talk nonstop in elevators while disguised in trench coat and dark glasses. He's also been known to attach toilet paper rolls to his feet and howl on traffic-jammed freeways.

Notice your reaction to some of Metcalf's actions. Did you find yourself thinking, "I could never do that"? Be assured that your resistance has shut down the creative part of your brain. If you want to open it back up, it's essential to overcome this block. Try the following exercises to get started.

Exercises

Exercise #1: Wear two different socks to the office.

Exercise #2: Stand backwards in an elevator.

Exercise #3: Go shopping in a Groucho Marx nose and glasses.

Exercise #4: Make a list of a dozen silly, absurd, totally ridiculous things you could do. And then do them!!!

1. _____

_____

2. _____

_____

3. _____

_____

26

4. _____

_____

5. _____

_____

6. _____

_____

7. _____

_____

8. _____

_____

9. _____

_____

10. _____

_____

11. _____

_____

12. _____

_____

New and Improved!

Block #2:

The "Don't Wear White Before Memorial Day" Syndrome A.K.A. Fear of breaking the rules

"Biggest liar in the world is 'they say.'"

—*Douglas Fairbanks*

"To know what you prefer, instead of humbly saying 'Amen' to what the world tells you you ought to prefer, is to have kept your soul alive."

—*Robert Louis Stevenson*

The teacher is probably impressed. You've been coloring between the lines all these years. How many rules do you follow blindly without even questioning why? Things like dress codes, eggs for breakfast, popcorn at movies.

Breaking through this block doesn't mean breaking rules for the sake of it—although it wouldn't hurt to practice for just a day. There are certainly helpful rules like speed limits and designated sides of the road to drive on. It's more about your ability to question rules and standards and decide whether they're really right for you. It's about going against the grain—if you need to.

Exercises

Exercise #1: Next time you're asked to write a fax or a memo, don't start with the traditional To: and From: format. Put these lines at the end or, better yet, in the middle. Write the memo from the bottom to the top of the page rather than from left to right. Or, if you just can't bring yourself to make this leap, at least create a new format for sending your memos.

Exercise #2: Get a coloring book and crayons and color to your heart's content. Outside the lines. Yes, this is somewhat childlike, but hey, isn't childhood when you were most creative?

Exercise #3: Wear something to work that breaks your personal dress code for the office.

Exercise #4: Make a list of twelve rules you'd enjoy breaking. Break them!!! (Remember, some rules are for your safety and that of others. And certainly don't break rules that will give you legal problems.)

1. _____

   _____

New and Improved!

2. _____

_____

3. _____

_____

4. _____

_____

5. _____

_____

6. _____

_____

7. _____

_____

8. _____

_____

9. _____

_____

10. _____

_____

11. _____

_____

12. _____

_____

Block #3:

The "But I'm Not Picasso" Syndrome
A.K.A. Fear of screwing up

"To live a creative life, we must lose our fear of being wrong."

—*Joseph Chilton Pearce*

It's important to give yourself permission to fail. Who told you it wasn't permissible to make mistakes? Truth is, making mistakes is essential. Have you ever noticed that when you make a mistake, it gives you a new perspective? If you're not making a couple of mistakes every day, you're not using your potential or growing as a person.

Jack Matson, a professor in Texas, teaches a class that has been nicknamed "Failure 101" because he encourages his students to do "impossible" things. The point? To learn from each mistake.

You've heard it before, but it's worth remembering: Edison tried more than a 1,000 different filaments before he invented the incandescent light bulb.

Reporters asked him, "How do you feel about failing that many times?"

He replied, "I didn't fail. Each time, I succeeded in finding a solution that didn't work."

Exercises

Exercise #1: Find a club or a bar with a karaoke machine. Sing your favorite song to your heart's content.

Exercise #2: Write a poem about your favorite relative and send it to a poetry magazine. Or write an editorial, a story, or an article for the company newsletter. The point is to write something creative and then submit it for public reading.

Exercise #3: Make a list of five titles for country songs.

Exercise #4: Make a sculpture out of clay. Display it proudly on your desk for several days.

Block #4:

The "Rodney Dangerfield" Syndrome
A.K.A. The enemy within

> "The sooner you all face up to the fact that you are lazy, untalented losers, unfit to kiss the feet of a genius like Friedrich Nietzsche, the better off you'll be."
>
> —*A professor in Matt Groening's comic strip,* School Is Hell

Sometimes our creativity gets stuck because we believe we're losers, nobodies. Secretly, we fear that if anybody got to really know us, if anybody peeked inside, they'd find a pretty pathetic person. We may be fooling other people, but we're not fooling ourselves.

These negative beliefs are probably your very biggest block. They can be bred by parents, religion, society, and fearful friends.

But take heed. Negative beliefs are just that. Beliefs. They're not facts. The world was never flat, although people once believed it to be so. The problem is, we tend to act the way we feel. If you've let others convince you that you're dumb, crazy, egomaniacal, you'll act that way. And acting the part will affirm to others that you are all those negative things. It's a vicious circle. These negative beliefs always go for the jugular. To overcome this block, do several of the exercises that follow.

Exercises

Exercise #1: Write down 100 of your best qualities.

Exercise #2: Recall three people who are old enemies of your creative self-worth. It's essential to acknowledge creative injuries and grieve them. Now, write each of these people a letter in your defense. Be as specific as possible. You might write something to the effect of "Dear Margaret Mary, Your breath smells like sewer slime and, by the way, I *can* draw." You don't need to mail these letters. Simply write them to acknowledge the injury. Go one step further and throw them away. With that action, you're dismissing those criticisms from your life.

Getting Out of Your Own Way

Exercise #3: Nurture yourself. It's okay to take some time for yourself each day. In fact, you'll find that you're able to deal with people and situations more effectively when you've taken care of your own needs.

Exercise #4: Create one wonderful smell in your house, simply because *you* like that smell.

Exercise #5: Wear your favorite item of clothing for no special occasion.

Exercise #6: List twenty things you enjoy doing (baking cookies, climbing trees, roller-blading). Next to each entry, pencil in the date you last let yourself do them. Don't be surprised if it's been years since you've done some of your favorites. Now set a new date for doing each activity and do them!!

1. _____

2. _____

3. _____

4. _____

5. _____

6. _____

7. _____

8. _____

New and Improved!

9. _____

10. _____

11. _____

12. _____

13. _____

14. _____

15. _____

16. _____

17. _____

18. _____

19. _____

20. _____

Getting Out of Your Own Way

Block #5:
The "Day-Planner" Syndrome A.K.A. Constipated thinking

> "A mind too active is no mind at all."
>
> —*Theodore Reothke*

What if someone suggested that you go to the library, check out *War and Peace,* and read it by tomorrow morning?

"What?!" you'd undoubtedly think. "I don't have time to read the newspaper, let alone some 1,067-page novel."

How true for most of us. This example drives home the point that we have become too busy. Our "To Do" lists grow by the day. And we become so obsessed with all these little errands and tasks that we don't take time for silent reflection.

The fact is, our life-style is often a big productivity killer. Most of us are simply too busy to be creative. Our minds are muddled with trivial details. Our creativity is literally clogged up with worries about what we're going to make for supper or how we're going to muster the nerve to ask off for the week of Memorial Day. We have "brain garbage." A good idea couldn't find its way in if it tried.

But consider this: Albert Einstein was daydreaming when he came up with the theory of relativity.

Exercise

Unexercise #1: Do nothing. Schedule an hour to do nothing. This means not reading, not watching TV, not doing anything, just sitting.

Unexercise #2: Give yourself time to listen to one side of an album you like, just for the joy of it. Notice how just twenty minutes can refresh you.

38

Block #6:

The "Syrup on Pancakes" Syndrome
A.K.A. Habitual thinking

> "When I have something to say that is too difficult for adults, I write for children. They have not closed the shutters. They like it when you rock the boat."

> —*Madeleine L'Engle*

One Christmas, a man asked his wife why she always cut both ends off the ham before basting it and sticking it in the oven. She replied, "Why, I don't know, that's how my mother always did it."

Since his wife's mother was coming for dinner later that day, he decided to investigate further. "Mom, why do you always cut both ends off the ham?" She, too, said, "It's what my mother always did."

New and Improved!

The man's curiosity got the better of him and he called his wife's grandmother to inquire about the mystery of the endless ham.

"Oh, that's simple. I cut the ends off because my pan was too small."

Are you sure you like eggs and bacon in the morning? Would you rather have cordon bleu or chocolate mousse?

When it comes to creativity, our habits are always suspect. We do them without thinking—and they don't always allow us to go where we might need to go. Like the ham in the story, they're often rituals we've adopted without question.

Even good habits confine us, especially when we're trying to come up with creative solutions. They inhibit us from traveling in new directions.

The good news? You can consciously overcome them. But you must become more of a novice than you're perhaps used to being. For example, if you want to change your golf swing, you can study the swing of an expert, but while you're learning to duplicate it, your golf game will suffer for awhile.

To overcome habits, we must have humility.

Exercises

Exercise #1: Eat a sandwich for breakfast and cornflakes for lunch.

Exercise #2: Put your shoes on differently. If you normally put the right one on first, switch to the left.

Exercise #3: Go upstairs with your right foot first instead of your left one. Or vice versa.

Exercise #4: Put your jacket on with the opposite sleeve first.

Exercise #5: Read a section of the paper you've never read before.

Exercise #6: Listen to a different radio station.

Exercise #7: Switch brands of toothpaste.

So how did you do? Don't despair if you haven't overcome all your blocks. We all have them—even pros do, although they probably wouldn't admit it. The point of these exercises is simply to become aware of blocks that might be holding you back and to make a conscious effort to move past your comfort zone. The more you practice doing things that are a little bit uncomfortable, the easier it will become and the more you'll wonder: "Why didn't I try this ages ago? Why have I been so scared?"

Just remember:

> ## "We learn to do something by doing it. There is no other way."

> *—John Holt, Educator*

Following are several additional exercises for activating your creative nature. None of these exercises is time-consuming or difficult. All they require is an open mind and the willingness to have a little fun. If you enjoyed the last exercises, you'll enjoy these. Remember, we learn by doing. The important thing is to keep practicing.

- Eat lunch somewhere you've never eaten—in a tree or under a bridge.

- Make five styles of paper airplanes and see which flies best.

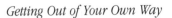

- Design a new coffee cup.

- Stage a poetry reading around a campfire.

- Make a piece of art from birdseed.

- Pull something from the trash and make something out of it.

- Paint a wall in your house—with artwork—not white paint.

42

- Go to the library and learn about crickets. Or something that's always fascinated you but you've never taken the time to learn about.

- Buy a gift for less than $1 and wrap it as expensively as possible.

- Make some ethnic food you've never made or tried before.

- Build a sand castle.

- Make sugar cookies shaped like body parts.

- Invent a new kind of pizza.

- Buy a CD that hasn't made the pop charts.

- Find the best vantage point for watching the sunset.

- Go to a restaurant and order dessert.

- Have a picnic at the park for breakfast.

- Get the most important person you know on the telephone.

- Get up at 3 a.m. to see what's on television.

- Make a balloon animal.

- Buy the most outrageous outfit at a thrift store.

- Go to a deserted field and dance.

New and Improved!

5

Flexing Your Creative Muscle: Eight Techniques for Pumping Up Your Brain

"The universe is full of magical things patiently waiting for our wits to grow sharper."

—*Eden Phillpotts*

*N*ow that you've worked through the blocks to your creativity, it's time to pump up your creative muscle—your brain. This section is chock-full of techniques and exercises for doing just that. But if you're like most people, you'll read through them once and think something like, "You know, that might just work" and then never do another thing about it. It's important to make these exercises a priority.

Getting creative takes time. It takes work. It takes discipline. It takes systematic behavior modification.

Remember, your brain wants to follow traditional patterns. It's trying to simplify your life by using things that have worked before.

Make a conscious effort to push yourself into foreign territory, to pursue new directions. The exercise that follows each technique will get you started doing just that.

The main thing is to take your pursuit of creativity seriously. Set aside a particular time and place every day to

New and Improved!

practice. Eliminate all distractions. Remember, this is important stuff. It doesn't have to take hours. Give yourself fifteen minutes every morning. Or a half hour right before dinner. The choice is yours, but be sure to schedule it into your life the way you'd schedule an aerobic workout or a tennis match.

What you put into these exercises is what you'll get out of them.

Have fun!!!!!

46

Technique #1:

Take your imagination to new heights.

> "The world of reality has its limits: the world of imagination is boundless."
>
> —*Jean-Jacques Rousseau*

More than likely, you underestimate the organ that sits inside your noggin. If you're like most people, you've probably said at some time or another:

"But I just don't get ideas."

"I don't have much of an imagination."

Au contraire! Your mind is very capable of creating and being imaginative. There's nothing more powerful than your own thoughts. In your mind, you can move through time and space—you can exercise your senses, emotions, and imagination far more freely than in the outer world.

Exercise

Ready! Begin.

First, take a deep breath, and try to totally relax. Feel your body going limp as you relax first your toes, then

New and Improved!

your legs, your trunk, your arms and fingers, your neck, and your face. Feel the tension flow out. Imagine a river carrying the day's worries from you. Picture yourself on a raft peacefully winding through a mountainous gorge. What do you see? wildflowers on the bank? white puffy clouds overhead? What do you hear? Smell?

Now we're going to crank it up a bit. You've hit white water. Can you feel the cold spray of water on your arms, your face? Can you see the mist settle in the hairs along your arm? Can you feel your muscles working as you maneuver around rocks and struggle to keep the raft on course? Uh-oh. Watch out! Here comes the waterfall. Can you feel your body stiffen and your eyes close as you plunge over the top?

Now open your eyes (in your mind). Where are you? Imagine that in your ride over the waterfall, you were jettisoned into outer space. You're floating aimlessly among celestial bodies. Is it cold and dark, or are you blinded by the radiance of the stars? Do you feel a melting heat?

Now let's bring things back down to earth. Imagine your favorite vacation spot. Conjure up the details. What does it look like? Relive the most favorite thing you did the last time you went there. Now imagine someplace you've never been but would like to go. What does it look like? What will you do? Who will you go with?

Next, let's try to experimenting with taste. Pick out the juiciest, plumpest strawberry from your mind's strawberry patch. Examine the strawberry. Decide what you want to do with it. Maybe you'd like it straight. Or with a pound of whipped cream.

Think of your favorite childhood activity. What made it your favorite? the people you were with? where it took place? the feeling you got from doing it?

Picture yourself doing it again. Now imagine something terrible happening as you do it. Make yourself think about the details. Now pretend it was a dream. Wake up. How do you feel? Happy? confused? exhausted?

Now, imagine something you've always wanted to do, but couldn't for some reason or another. Go all out. Don't let time, money, or other commitments stop you. Will you take a night-time limousine ride down Broadway in New York? Attend an Oscar party? Get the promotion you've always wanted?

And you said you weren't creative!

Technique #2:
Make unusual associations.

"If I have ever made any valuable
discoveries, it has been owing
more to patient attention, than
to any other talent."

—*Isaac Newton*

The ability to make unusual associations is vital to
creative thinking. For example, Bill Bowerman, the
man who invented Nike shoes, was sitting at
breakfast one morning trying to come up with a better
running shoe. He happened to notice his wife's waffle
iron. The rest, as they say, is history.

51

Exercise

Now you try it! Take the first word on any consecutive twenty-five pages of the dictionary. Write a story using those words.

_____ _____

_____ _____

_____ _____

_____ _____

_____ _____

_____ _____

_____ _____

_____ _____

Technique #3:

Set an idea quota.

"Getting ideas is like shaving; if you don't do it every day, you're a bum."

—*Alex Kroll, Advertising Executive*

Come up with ten new ideas every day. Maybe one of your ideas would be seatbelts for dogs. Another might be a movie theater with beds—so you can really relax.

The point is not to restrict yourself to ideas that are practical. Or ideas that you know will work. The point is to practice using your brain—the same way doing sit-ups practices your body. You don't do sit-ups so you can win a sit-up competition. You do them so your body will be in better shape. That's how this exercise works. Do it for the workout it will give your brain.

Don't force yourself to think of ideas. Let them come from things you see and hear along the roadside or on television. If you train your brain to make the unusual associations described in Technique #2, you'll find yourself surpassing your idea quota each day. Remember to write your ideas down. It's always helpful to keep a journal.

Nobel Prize winner Linus Pauling said, "The best way to get a good idea is to get a lot of ideas."

Exercise

Get started now. Write down ten ideas for today.

1. _____

2. _____

3. _____

4. _____

5. _____

6. _____

7. _____

8. _____

9. _____

10. _____

Technique #4:
Write lists to brainstorm ideas.

"Nothing is more dangerous than an idea, when you have only one idea."

—Emile Chartier (Alain),
French philosopher

Making lists is a valuable exercise for pumping up your creative muscle—as long as you push yourself a little. For example, writing down five uses for a chocolate chip cookie may not get you past your comfort zone, but by number thirteen or fourteen,

you'll be inventing everything from Frisbee substitutes to bathtub toys. By this time, you'll be forced into alternative thinking.

Another good way to write a list is to give yourself a set time period (say five minutes) and make as long a list as possible. This will keep your brain running fluidly.

By now, you've probably figured out that making lists in this way is sometimes called brainstorming. Businesses use this technique all the time to come up with creative solutions and ideas. The important thing is to keep the ideas flowing. Don't stop to censor or edit anything you write down. The whole point is to get lots of ideas that you can later weed out. Sometimes the good ideas emerge only after you've gotten rid of a lot of junk. Most of us cut ourselves off before we've allowed the junk to air. Junk needs a voice too, and the more you let it out, the less obnoxious it will be. Remember, being creative is giving yourself permission to come up with bad ideas as well.

Exercises

Exercise #1: Make a list of 100 ways to clean the bathroom.

Exercise #2: Make a list of 25 things to make lists of.

Exercise #3: Get a group together. Write your problem or question clearly. Start throwing out ideas, the more the better. Don't stop until you have 1,000 different suggestions. Start with ideas that are red. Then move to ideas that won't work. Ideas that would work only in a particular situation. Give an award for the most ridiculous idea.

Technique 5:

Design some gimmicks.

> "If you do not expect the
> unexpected, you will not find it."
>
> —*Heraclitus, Greek philosopher*

Gimmicks divert your mind from taking its usual
course. A simple gimmick suggested by George
Prince is to open a book, put your finger blindly on a
word, and use that word in the
process of
creating a new
concept. For
example, if you
want to figure out a
way to increase sales in
Nebraska, open a book and put your finger on a word.

You may not get your answer, but you *will* exercise
your mind as you attempt to use the word to solve
your sales problem.

New and Improved!

Exercise

1. Write down a problem you'd like to solve, a challenge you'd like to meet.

   _____

   _____

   _____

2. Close this book. Then open it, pointing blindly at any word on the open page.

   Write the word here. _____

   _____

   Now use it to try to resolve the issue you described in #1.

   _____

   _____

   _____

   _____

   _____

   _____

   _____

   _____

Technique #6:

Use your "imagine-ation" to manipulate familiar images.

> "You cannot depend on your eyes when your imagination is out of focus."
>
> —*Mark Twain*

Sampson Raphaelson, a famous playwright of the 1930s and 1940s and a screenwriter of the first talking movie, defined imagination as "the capacity to see what is there."

But sometimes what we "see" becomes entirely too familiar—clichéd, if you will. We form one-sided images and never "look" beyond them. Often, we're just out of practice with consciously eliciting images with *all* our senses. Sometimes all we need to do to see a familiar image in a new way is to focus on a different sense as we think about the image. For example, if you immediately see trees when someone says the word *forest,* perhaps you should try imagining the smell of wet rabbit fur instead. Eventually, you'll get a much fuller image of *forest* as you imagine it with each of your senses.

Exercise

Imagine each of the following and notice whether you
are more attuned to one type of sensory imagery
than another:

- A pink rose

- The voice of Madonna

- The smell of summer
  barbecue grills

- The smoothness of a baby's
  bottom

- The sound of a bee

- The sweetness of a lump of sugar

Now try manipulating your imagination. Imagine:

- A cat riding a bicycle

- Purple ice cubes dancing the tango

- A lawnmower singing Madonna

You can improve your imagination by having fun with
images you already know.

Technique #7:

Race against another person to come up with creative ideas.

> "Ideas are the factors that lift civilization. They create revolutions. There is more dynamite in an idea than in many bombs."
>
> —*John H. Vincent*

This is a variation of techniques #3 and #4. Find someone who's willing to play the idea quota game with you. Have a race to see who can come up with fifteen ideas first. When you're racing against the clock or another person, you don't give yourself time to judge. Your mind doesn't have time to say, "but it will never work."

Exercises

1. Write down fifteen uses for a detached shoe tongue.

2. Come up with fifteen ways to lure a boa out of a bin of Idaho potatoes.

3. If you were a sponge, what would be your favorite mess? Write down fifteen possibilities.

New and Improved!

Technique #8:

Look at life with fresh, amazed eyes.

"Science does not know its debt to imagination."

—Ralph Waldo Emerson

Part of the problem we have as adults is that we've lost our ability to really look at the world. As adults, we get so caught up in our routines that we forget to look out the window on the way to work. We forget to notice the bank teller's magnetic eyes or the flower growing brazenly between two bricks in the sidewalk. Today, make it a point to really think about things, to look at your life and appreciate the wonder that it is. Open yourself to the moment. Otherwise, you'll just continue to create more of what you've already done in your life. If you're thinking B-O-R-I-N-G or, worse yet, if you're not thinking a single thing, consider some of the amazing things that follow:

1. Delivery from California to New York, overnight

2. A forest—think about all the life forms it supports

3. An octopus—imagine having all those legs

4. The United States telephone system—have you ever faxed anyone in Papua New Guinea?

5. ATM machines—money in Connecticut when your bank is in Nebraska

6. A daisy—simplicity at its finest

Aren't all those things pretty amazing? We are surrounded everyday by the products of nature and of our own imaginations, of human creativity. They serve as reminders of what we can accomplish if we only open ourselves to the realm of possibility.

Okay, so you're starting to get the picture. You're beginning to pump up that old brain. The cobwebs are gone. The juice is starting to flow. Remember to keep going with your list-making. And your ideas. If you continue to think of ten each day, within a year, you'll have more than 3,000 ideas. Who knows? Maybe one of them might even make you a million dollars. Perhaps your next step is to develop some exercises so that you can use at least one idea each day. Remember, you're the creative one here.

6

Aha! Eleven Ideas for Looking at Challenges in New Ways

"Originality is simply a fresh pair of eyes."

—*Thomas Wentworth Higginson*

*T*he eleven techniques suggested in this chapter are designed to help you work through challenges that aren't responding to your old ways of doing things.

Say you want to boost sales in Rhode Island but the salesmen are complaining that the market is oversaturated. Try any one of these techniques to come up with a solution.

Or maybe you want to design a new product that your company can sell along with its standbys. Again, these techniques can help.

It doesn't matter what your problem is. It might be a challenge at home. It might be a challenge at work. The point is that these tools will help you look at the challenge from a different viewpoint. Often, when you do, the solution will jump out at you.

Technique #1:

Perform an "attribute analysis."

"Ideas are the root of creation."

—*Ernest Dimnet*

If you want to change something that already exists, write down all the product's attributes. Take a desk, for example. It stores things. It gives you room to write. It hold books. It organizes files. It keeps you from other people. Next, come up with alternatives for each of the product's attributes. You'll be surprised at the new uses you'll find for the product.

Exercise

Product

_____

Attribute	Alternative
_____	_____
_____	_____
_____	_____
_____	_____
_____	_____

Technique #2:

Seek advice entirely outside of your field.

> **"He that won't be counseled can't be helped."**
>
> —*Benjamin Franklin*

When you're trying to come up with creative solutions, don't forget to ask for the advice of people who aren't stuck in your particular mind-set. If you're looking for ways to increase sales, for example, ask a minister, a doctor, a bartender, or a Girl Scout.

Gerald Jampolsky, a psychiatrist, frequently takes his problems to children, who have much freer minds.

A hotel executive introduced pizza in his restaurants after talking to a sanitation worker who found pizza boxes in the hotel trash.

Exercise

Make a list of the people you meet casually each day
who could help you see a situation from a different
perspective (e.g., a mother of four could have
insightful advice for managing difficult people).

_____

_____

_____

_____

_____

_____

_____

_____

_____

_____

_____

_____

_____

_____

_____

Technique #3:

Play movie director with your dreams.

> ## "Creation is a drug I can't do without."

> —*Cecil B. DeMille*

Solutions to problems often come when we least expect them—after a certain "gestation" period. And dreams often provide answers to our challenges. Robert Louis Stevenson dreamed *Dr. Jekyll and Mr. Hyde.* Elias Howe, while trying to come up with a method for attaching thread to the needle of the sewing machine he invented, dreamed of cannibals with holes in their spears. Niels Borh dreamed a model of the atom.

You can coach yourself to receive dream images by asking your intuition: "Give me a dream about _____. Awaken me as soon as the dream is over."

With practice, you'll be able to dream and wake like this at will.

As soon as you're awake, don't open your

eyes. Instead, review your dream. Then open your eyes and get the pad and pencil you've left by your bedside and quickly write down the main elements of the dream.

The key is to write down the key images or words that come to mind as soon as you realize they are there. The insights can be hard to recapture, so take advantage of their first visit. Later you can fill in gaps and other details.

Exercise

Make a list of some problems you can coach yourself to dream about—then do it!

_____

_____

_____

_____

_____

_____

_____

_____

_____

_____

Technique #4:
Go for a walk.

"The value of an idea lives in the using of it."

—*Thomas Edison*

You're stuck. You've been racking your brain for what seems like an eternity. You just can't think of another possibility. As far as you're concerned, you might as well give up.

When defeat seems to be beckoning, don't give in. Instead, let go for awhile. File the idea away and go for a walk. It doesn't matter where—although a walk outdoors certainly will help get your mind off the problem.

The main thing is to go, leave, trusting that when you come back, the solution will be there.

It's important to let ideas incubate.

Technique #5:
Study nature.

"Man must go back to nature for information."

—*Thomas Paine*

When all else fails, remember there's a great creator—call it Mother Nature, God, whatever—that isn't too shabby when it comes to great ideas. If you can't think of a solution on your own, take a look around at what Mother Nature has come up with.

Alexander Graham Bell, for example, modeled the telephone after the human ear. The hypodermic needle was patterned after the fangs of a rattlesnake.

Technique #6:
Rediscover how to play.

> "New opinions are always suspected, and usually opposed, without any other reason but because they are not already common."

—*John Locke, English philosopher*

A recent study pointed out that only 2 percent of adults are creative. By comparison, 10 percent of seven-year-olds and 90 percent of five-years-olds are creative. Does this tell you anything? Part of the reason kids are so creative is they don't take themselves so darned seriously. If you're stuck on something, give yourself permission to goof off for a while. Quit worrying. If you don't remember how to play, buy a box of blocks and build a movie theater. Or see whether some of your co-workers will stage an impromptu production of *The Wizard of Oz*. Remember, this isn't brain surgery.

Again, it's important to note your reactions to taking some time off to play. Do you automatically censor this idea as childish, a waste of time? Have you already decided to put it on hold, thinking you'll do it later or after you've finished some important task?

These thoughts are important clues to how you rate creativity. You'll quickly realize where it ranks in your life.

Give yourself permission to play the next time you're faced with a challenge. You'll be surprised at what happens when you come back to your problem.

Einstein used to imagine riding beams of lights. Gallileo invented the telescope as a toy until he realized he could use it for other things.

Exercise

Buy yourself a yo-yo or something you liked as a kid. Play with it. Do you feel your mind loosening up, your creativity kicking in?

Technique #7:

Keep a notebook.

"You see things and you say 'Why?'; but I dream things that never were and I say 'Why not?'"

—*George Bernard Shaw*

Our brains can hold only five to nine pieces of information at any one time. That's why it's imperative to carry a journal and write your ideas down as soon as they come to you.

John Patterson, former president of NCR, was a fan of Napoleon. He not only rode horseback with his executives every day at 5 a.m., he also required them to carry a book to record their daily activities, thoughts, and ideas. He fired those who failed to maintain their books. Interestingly enough, one-sixth of the major U.S. companies were headed by former NCR executives in the early 1900s.

Buy yourself a notebook and carry it with you at all times. It doesn't have to be fancy—although your creative side may just want to decorate the cover. It doesn't have to be expensive—discount stores sell spiral notebooks for less than three dollars. But remember, give yourself a forum for expressing all that wonderful bottled-up creativity.

Technique #8:

Imagine yourself as the problem you'd like to solve.

"In differentiation, not in uniformity, lies the path of progress."

—*Louis Dembitz Brandeis,
U.S. Supreme Court Justice*

Unfortunately, we remove ourselves from problems in order to solve them. Often, it's more effective to do just the opposite: to become the problem.

Here's how it works:

1. Relax in a daydream state.

2. Free yourself from all inhibitions. If Einstein could do this, you can too.

3. Take on the attributes of the problem you're trying to solve. Become its color, taste, speed, texture, shape, and so on.

New and Improved!

4. Place what you have become into the desired situation. Notice your reactions.

5. Now record and analyze the results.

Remember, this is the exercise that created Silkience for the Gillette company. And Michael Faraday, founder of electromagnetic theory, pictured himself as an atom under pressure.

Technique #9:

Change the questions you are asking.

"The uncreative mind can spot wrong answers, but it takes a creative mind to spot wrong questions."

—Anthony Jay

If you have a challenge you can't seem to overcome, you may be beating yourself on the head with the same old questions. For example, if you're trying to figure out how to lower the bridge, maybe you should be asking how to raise the water. There are always new approaches to everything, and asking questions is the only way to get your brain to provide an answer. Whenever you pose a question, your brain immediately goes to work to come up with an answer. That's how the brain works. Maybe you haven't been asking the right questions.

Technique #10:

Create a bulletin board of directors.

"I ask questions. The stupidity of people comes from having an answer for everything. The wisdom of the novel comes from having a question for everything."

—*Milan Kundera*

This technique comes from the book *Thinkertoys* by Michael Michalko. In it, he recommends creating a fantasy board of powerhouse business leaders and innovators who will assist you in overcoming challenges. Imagine having at your disposal the experience, wisdom, and know-how of Thomas Edison, Albert Einstein, and Leonardo da Vinci.

Here's how it works.

1. Create a "creativity" board of directors that includes some of the people you most admire. Your fictitious board can include historical figures, modern-day celebrieties, and people you know personally.

2. Find photos of the people you've chosen to be on this estimable committee, or get inspirational quotes—anything to remind you of the pool of talent you now have to draw on. Pin these photos and quotes on your dashboard or in your office.

3. Why do these people stand out in your eyes? Is it because of the way they approached problems? Tackled challenges when prevailing wisdom doomed them to fail?

4. Every time you have a challenge, call a meeting of the members of your committee and imagine how they would solve it.

Exercise

Write down the names of several people who would be good candidates for your personal board of directors.

_____

_____

_____

_____

_____

_____

_____

Technique #11:
Practice reverse thinking.

> "Every man of genius sees the world at a different angle from his fellows."
>
> —*Havelock Ellis,*
> *English scientist and author*

This exercise frees your thinking from deeply embedded assumptions. Many creative thinkers get their most original ideas by challenging and reversing the obvious.

One CEO, for example, gave bonuses just *before* the company's busy season instead of after it.

Here are the major steps involved:

1. State your challenge.

2. List your assumptions about the challenge. This alone will help you clear out the cobwebs.

3. Challenge each assumption.

4. Reverse each assumption. Ask yourself how to accomplish each reversal.

5. Record differing viewpoints that might be useful to consider. List as many as you can.

82

Exercise

1. State a challenge you are facing.

   _____

   _____

   _____

   _____

   _____

   _____

2. Follow steps 2 to 5 in Technique #11 to solve the problem.

   _____

   _____

   _____

   _____

   _____

   _____

   _____

   _____

   _____

New and Improved!

7

Taking Your Act on the Road

"How monotone the sounds of the forest would be if the music came only from the top ten birds."

*L*ook how far you've come. By now, you've made creativity an important ritual in your life. You're starting to see how rusty your old brain had become. And how easy it really is to pump it back into shape.

Whatever you do, don't stop now. Make creative thinking a daily practice. And remember these final pointers:

1. We all have a great need to connect with ourselves. Creativity is one of the best ways to do that.

2. There are always hundreds of solutions to every challenge. If you think there is only one right answer, then you will stop looking as soon as you find one.

3. As you practice, don't make the results important.

4. Give yourself permission to be silly, to act foolish. Go ahead. Let down your guard.

5. Persevere. As Kermit the Frog, says "It ain't easy being green."

And, finally, for those times when your creativity is really in need of a boost, here are some fun facts about America's mothers and fathers of invention you can turn to for inspiration.

- Any grade schooler knows that Thomas Edison invented the light bulb, the phonograph, and the movie projector. But it's a rare American indeed who knows that the patron saint of ingenuity also concocted a four-car garage with a turntable so he wouldn't have to back out.

- Hedy Lamarr, infamous silver screen sex symbol, was also an inventor. Her 1942 patent for an antijamming device (it's still being used) was given to the American government as her contribution to the war effort. An Austrian by birth, Lamarr first gained notoriety for running naked through the woods in a 1933 Czech film. She used her $500, seven-year contract with Hollywood's MGM to put an ocean between herself and Hitler. Lamarr used her head for more than just anti-Nazi devices. One such invention received the help of Howard Hughes, who lent her a pair of chemists to develop a bouillon-like cube which, when mixed with water, created a Coca-Cola clone.

- Abraham Lincoln, besides penning eloquent speeches, landed a patent for a boat that enabled the sailor to cross ground without getting out of the boat.

- B.F. Goodrich, whose chief occupation was tires, also invented a billiard table with side rails.

- Long before the water bed was invented, J. Foster came up with a floating bed complete with oars and a drawer for storing provisions. Other unusual beds include Samuel S. Applegate's 1882 alarm bed that aroused sleeping beauties by plunking them in the head with sixty corks, and Ludwig Ederer's 1900 wake-up wonder that actually tilted the bed upright until sleepers careened to the floor.

- Although they didn't have Nikes at the turn of the century, overplump chickens, in order to get their feed, were forced to jog (or at least move on the spinning platform) in William J. Manly's 1906 hen exerciser. Another fowl innovation was concocted by Andrew Jackson in 1903. (No, not that Andrew Jackson!) His idea? Chicken sunglasses.

- If Whistler's Mother had only known! Before the electric motor, inventors relied on rocking chairs to churn butter (1913), play accordions, and power everything from fans (1869) to washing machines (1890).

New and Improved!

- U.S. Patent 285,144 might not work for major-league shortstop Ozzie Smith, but it sure comes in handy for his fans. Catch-a-Cap, which looks like an everyday baseball cap, is perfect for high pop fouls heading for the stands. Thanks to four finger loops, this new invention doubles as a baseball mitt.

- It's a bird! It's a plane! No, it's Paul Moller's flying saucer. The Dixon, California, engineer who built his first I.F.O. (that's identified flying object) in 1964 is still perfecting a saucer that at last sighting rose forty feet into the air.

Bibliography & Suggested Resources

Adams, James L. *Conceptual Blockbusting: A Guide to Better Ideas.* Reading, MA: Addison-Wesley, 1986.

Adams, James L. *The Care and Feeding of Ideas: A Guide to Encouraging Creativity.* Reading, MA: Addison-Wesley, 1986.

Blohowiak, Donald. *Mavericks! How to Lead Your Staff to Think Like Einstein, Create Like da Vinci and Invent Like Edison.* Homewood, IL: Business One Irwin, 1992.

Cohen, Daniel. *Creativity: What Is It?* New York: M. Evans and Company, 1977.

Glover, John A. *Becoming a More Creative Person.* Englewood Cliffs, NJ: Prentice-Hall, 1980.

Hanks, Kurt, and Jay A. Parry. *Wake Up Your Creative Genius.* Los Altos, CA: William Kaufmann, 1983.

John-Steiner, Vera. *Notebooks of the Mind: Explorations of Thinking.* New York: Perennial Library, 1985.

Keil, John M. *How to Zig in a Zagging World: Unleashing Your Hidden Creativity.* New York: John Wiley & Sons, 1988.

Keil, John M. *The Creative Mystique: How to Manage It, Nurture It, and Make It Pay.* New York: John Wiley & Sons, 1985.

Michalko, Michael. *Thinkertoys: A Handbook of Business Creativity for the '90s.* Berkley, CA: Ten Speed Press, 1991.

Miller, William C. *The Creative Edge: Fostering Innovation Where You Work.* Reading, MA: Addison-Wesley, 1987.

Nayak, P. Ranganath, and John M. Ketteringham. *Breakthroughs.* New York: Rawson Associates, 1986.

Norins, Hanley. *The Young and Rubicam Traveling Creative Workshop.* New York: Prentice-Hall, 1990.

Raudsepp, Eugene. *Creative Growth Games.* New York: Perigee, 1980.

Raudsepp, Eugene. *How Creative Are You?* New York: Perigee, 1981.

New and Improved!

Ray, Michael, and Rochelle Myers. *Creativity in Business.* Garden City, NY: Doubleday, 1986.

SARK. *Inspiration Sandwich.* Celestial Arts, 1992.

Stanish, Bob. *Mindanderings: Creative Classroom Approaches to Thinking, Writing and Problem Solving.* Carthage, IL: Good Apple, 1990.

Von Oech, Roger. *A Kick in the Seat of the Pants: Using Your Explorer, Artist, Judge, and Warrior to Be More Creative.* New York: Perennial Library, 1986.

Upton, Albert, Richard Samson, and Ann Dahlstrom Farmer. *Creative Analysis.* New York: E.P. Dutton, 1978.

Williams, Robert H., and John Stockmyer. *Unleashing the Right Side of the Brain: The LARC Creativity Program.* Lexington, MA: The Stephen Greene Press, 1987.

Worthy, Morgan. *Aha: A Puzzle Approach to Creative Thinking.* Chicago: Nelson Hall, 1975.

Available From SkillPath Publications

Self-Study Sourcebooks

Climbing the Corporate Ladder: What You Need to Know and Do to Be a Promotable Person *by Barbara Pachter and Marjorie Brody*

Coping With Supervisory Nightmares: 12 Common Nightmares of Leadership and What You Can Do About Them *by Michael and Deborah Singer Dobson*

Defeating Procrastination: 52 Fail-Safe Tips for Keeping Time on Your Side *by Marlene Caroselli, Ed.D.*

Discovering Your Purpose *by Ivy Haley*

Going for the Gold: Winning the Gold Medal for Financial Independence *by Lesley D. Bissett, CFP*

Having Something to Say When You Have to Say Something: The Art of Organizing Your Presentation *by Randy Horn*

Info-Flood: How to Swim in a Sea of Information Without Going Under *by Marlene Caroselli, Ed.D.*

The Innovative Secretary *by Marlene Caroselli, Ed.D.*

Letters and Memos: Just Like That! *by Dave Davies*

Mastering the Art of Communication: Your Keys to Developing a More Effective Personal Style *by Michelle Fairfield Poley*

Organized for Success! 95 Tips for Taking Control of Your Time, Your Space, and Your Life *by Nanci McGraw*

A Passion to Lead! How to Develop Your Natural Leadership Ability *by Michael Plumstead*

P.E.R.S.U.A.D.E.: Communication Strategies That Move People to Action *by Marlene Caroselli, Ed.D.*

Productivity Power: 250 Great Ideas for Being More Productive *by Jim Temme*

Promoting Yourself: 50 Ways to Increase Your Prestige, Power, and Paycheck *by Marlene Caroselli, Ed.D.*

Proof Positive: How to Find Errors Before They Embarrass You *by Karen L. Anderson*

Risk-Taking: 50 Ways to Turn Risks Into Rewards *by Marlene Caroselli, Ed.D. and David Harris*

Stress Control: How You Can Find Relief From Life's Daily Stress *by Steve Bell*

The Technical Writer's Guide *by Robert McGraw*

Total Quality Customer Service: How to Make It Your Way of Life *by Jim Temme*

Write It Right! A Guide for Clear and Correct Writing *by Richard Andersen and Helene Hinis*

Your Total Communication Image *by Janet Signe Olson, Ph.D.*

Handbooks

The ABC's of Empowered Teams: Building Blocks for Success *by Mark Towers*

Breaking the Ice: How to Improve Your On-the-Spot Communication Skills *by Deborah Shouse*

The Care and Keeping of Customers: A Treasury of Facts, Tips and Proven Techniques for Keeping Your Customers Coming BACK! *by Roy Lantz*

Challenging Change: Five Steps for Dealing With Change *by Holly DeForest and Mary Steinberg*

Dynamic Delegation! A Manager's Guide For Active Empowerment *by Mark Towers*

Every Woman's Guide to Career Success *by Denise M. Dudley*

Exploring Personality Styles: A Guide for Better Understanding Yourself and Your Colleagues *by Michael Dobson*

Grammar? No Problem! *by Dave Davies*

Great Openings and Closings: 28 Ways to Launch and Land Your Presentations With Punch, Power, and Pizazz *by Mari Pat Varga*

Hiring and Firing: What Every Manager Needs to Know *by Marlene Caroselli, Ed.D. with Laura Wyeth, Ms.Ed.*

How to Be a More Effective Group Communicator: Finding Your Role and Boosting Your Confidence in Group Situations *by Deborah Shouse*

How to Deal With Difficult People *by Paul Friedman*

Learning to Laugh at Work: The Power of Humor in the Workplace *by Robert McGraw*

Making Your Mark: How to Develop a Personal Marketing Plan for Becoming More Visible and More Appreciated at Work *by Deborah Shouse*

Meetings That Work *by Marlene Caroselli, Ed.D.*

The Mentoring Advantage: How to Help Your Career Soar to New Heights *by Pam Grout*

Minding Your Business Manners: Etiquette Tips for Presenting Yourself Professionally in Every Business Situation *by Marjorie Brody and Barbara Pachter*

Misspeller's Guide *by Joel and Ruth Schroeder*

Motivation in the Workplace: How to Motivate Workers to Peak Performance and Productivity *by Barbara Fielder*

NameTags Plus: Games You Can Play When People Don't Know What to Say *by Deborah Shouse*

Networking: How to Creatively Tap Your People Resources *by Colleen Clarke*

New & Improved! 25 Ways to Be More Creative and More Effective *by Pam Grout*

Power Write! A Practical Guide to Words That Work *by Helene Hinis*

The Power of Positivity: Eighty Ways to energize your life *by Joel and Ruth Schroeder*

Putting Anger to Work For You! *by Ruth and Joel Schroeder*

Reinventing Your Self: 28 Strategies for Coping With Change *by Mark Towers*

The Supervisor's Guide: The Everyday Guide to Coordinating People and Tasks *by Jerry Brown and Denise Dudley, Ph.D.*

Taking Charge: A Personal Guide to Managing Projects and Priorities *by Michal E. Feder*

Treasure Hunt: 10 Stepping Stones to a New and More Confident You! *by Pam Grout*

A Winning Attitude: How to Develop Your Most Important Asset! *by Michelle Fairfield Poley*

For more information, call 1-800-873-7545.